# Daily Prayer
## Drawing Near the Throne of Grace

*(Praying through Hebrews)*

*Berenice Aguilera*

For my Church

Check out
www.bereniceaguilera.com
for your free copy of
Daily Prayer through the Ten Commandments.

# Table of Contents

# Introduction

The letter of Hebrews is overflowing with encouragement to persevere in faith and enter into God's rest. It teaches so much about Jesus and is so personal in nature that you will find yourself wanting, more than anything, to grow in the knowledge of God.

God's word is living and active. You can't read it, and pray through it, without the mighty work of our holy God working in and through you.

At times you will worship and praise.

Other times your jaw will drop at understanding something that pierces deep into your heart (often from familiar passages you have read before).

And yet other times you will find yourself on your knees repenting and asking forgiveness.

As you begin to read, imagine you are the recipient of the letter. What is God's word saying to you? Ask God to open your spiritual eyes, and to give you wisdom and knowledge.

After each scripture reading is a prayer. Begin with the written prayer, then bring before God whatever comes to mind next. Whether praise and thanksgiving, worship, repentance or petition. Bring it all before Him, because you are His child, and He loves you.

As you pray each day, you will begin to notice a deepening of your relationship with Him.

There is no greater experience in life than looking to God, being changed by Him, and hearing Him speak to you through His word.

May God bless you as you seek Him.

# God has spoken...

## Hebrews 1:1-6

*God, having in the past spoken to the fathers through the prophets at many times and in various ways, has at the end of these days spoken to us by his Son, whom he appointed heir of all things, through whom also he made the worlds.*

*His Son is the radiance of his glory, the very image of his substance, and upholding all things by the word of his power, who, when he had by himself purified us of our sins, sat down on the right hand of the Majesty on high, having become as much better than the angels as the more excellent name he has inherited is better than theirs.*

*For to which of the angels did he say at any time,*

*"You are my Son.  Today I have become your father?"*

*and again,*

*"I will be to him a Father, and he will be to me a Son?*

*When he again brings in the firstborn into the world he says, Let all the angels of God worship him.*

O Lord you have searched me and you know me, you know when I sit and when I rise, you perceive my thoughts from afar, you discern my going out and my lying down, you are familiar with all my ways.

You O Lord are the radiance of God's glory and you sustain all things through the power of your word. You have provided cleansing for sin and sat down at the right hand of the Father Almighty.  You reign!

You who are so great in wonder, made yourself known to us by the power of your Spirit.  May your name be glorified and lifted up in all the earth.

May your majesty and holiness be manifest among your people, to the praise of your glory. Amen.

# Your throne, O God, is forever

## Hebrews 1:7-14

*Of the angels he says, He makes his
angels winds, and his servants a flame of
fire. But of the Son he says,*

*Your throne, O God, is forever and ever.
The sceptre of uprightness is the sceptre
of your Kingdom. You have loved
righteousness and hated iniquity;
therefore God, your God, has anointed
you with the oil of gladness above your
fellows.*

*And,*

*You, Lord, in the beginning, laid the
foundation of the earth. The heavens are
the works of your hands. They will
perish, but you continue. They all will
grow old like a garment does. You will*

*roll them up like a mantle, and they will be changed; but you are the same. Your years won't fail.*

*But which of the angels has he told at any time, Sit at my right hand, until I make your enemies the footstool of your feet? Aren't they all serving spirits, sent out to do service for the sake of those who will inherit salvation?*

The Lord reigns! Let the earth rejoice for righteousness and justice are the foundation of His throne. There is no-one like you, whose every enemy will bow before you.

You make yourself known throughout the earth, and all creation sings praise to the power of your name. Your throne, O God will last forever. You are from everlasting to everlasting.

O, how my soul sings your praise, and my mind rejoices in the surety of your salvation. My foundation is based on your righteousness, and the truth of your word.

You have saved me. You have washed my sin away as far as the East is from the West and I live in the hope you have given me. Amen.

# Pay close attention

## Hebrews 2:1-4

*Therefore we ought to pay greater attention to the things that were heard, lest perhaps we drift away.*

*For if the word spoken through angels proved steadfast, and every transgression and disobedience received a just penalty, how will we escape if we neglect so great a salvation - which at the first having been spoken through the Lord, was confirmed to us by those who heard, God also testifying with them, both by signs and wonders, by various works of power and by gifts of the Holy Spirit, according to his own will?*

Lord Jesus, you said that if I obey your commands I will remain in your love. This is what I want for my life.

You have saved me and I trust in you. Help me to pay more careful attention to your word. I ask for increasing desire and dependence on your word in my life.

You said, 'man cannot live by bread alone, but by every word that comes from the mouth of the Lord.'

I know that I cannot live without your word. There is no nightmare greater than the thought of drifting away from you.

Soften my heart O God, and give me grace every day to live a life marked by your love for me. Help me to love as you love, in Jesus name, amen.

# We see Jesus

## Hebrews 2:5-9

*For he didn't subject the world to come, of which we speak, to angels. But one has somewhere testified, saying,*

*"What is man, that you think of him? Or the son of man, that you care for him? You made him a little lower than the angels. You crowned him with glory and honor. You have put all things in subjection under his feet."*

*For in that he subjected all things to him, he left nothing that is not subject to him. But now we don't see all things subjected to him, yet. But we see him who has been made a little lower than the angels, Jesus, because of the suffering of death crowned with glory and honor, that by the grace of God he should taste of death for everyone.*

Lord Jesus, the kingdom of this world has become your kingdom, and you reign for ever and ever. You are crowned with glory and honour, majesty and power and everything is subject to you.

You triumphed over death on the cross, bringing life to all the Father has given you. O Lord, what amazing grace and love you extend towards us. What fullness of life and hope you have filled us with.

With all of creation I declare, worthy is the Lamb who was slain, to receive power and wealth and wisdom and strength and honour and glory and praise!

To him who sits on the throne and to the Lamb be praise and honour, and glory and power, for ever and ever! Amen.

# Being made holy

## Hebrews 2:10-14

*For it became him, for whom are all
things, and through whom are all things,
in bringing many children to glory, to
make the author of their salvation perfect
through sufferings.*

*For both he who sanctifies and those
who are sanctified are all from one, for
which cause he is not ashamed to call
them brothers, saying,*

*"I will declare your name to my brothers.
Among the congregation I will sing your
praise."*

*Again, "I will put my trust in him."*
*Again, "Behold, here I am with the*
*children whom God has given me."*

*Since then the children have shared in*
*flesh and blood, he also himself in the*
*same way partook of the same, that*
*through death he might bring to nothing*
*him who had the power of death, that is,*
*the devil...*

Thank you Lord that you have saved me from the consequences of sin and death. Thank you that I belong to you and that you are making me holy.

I am one of the children the Father has given you. I can barely grasp the implications of such grace extended to me, such pure love poured over me. I was once dead but you gave me life, you adopted me and set your Holy Spirit upon me as a seal guaranteeing my future.

Lord Jesus, you are not ashamed of me. My heart longs to please you. Such divine favour has rested over my life. I want to change. I want to please you.

Lord, I pray for humility of heart, submitting to you in everything. Even as you loved and obeyed the Father, I also want to love and obey you.

Change my heart. Change my mind and thinking to be more like you. I ask this in Jesus name, amen.

# Merciful and faithful High Priest

## Hebrews 2:15-18

*...and might deliver all of them who through fear of death were all their lifetime subject to bondage. For most certainly, he doesn't give help to angels, but he gives help to the offspring of Abraham.*

*Therefore he was obligated in all things to be made like his brothers, that he might become a merciful and faithful high priest in things pertaining to God, to make atonement for the sins of the people.*

*For in that he himself has suffered being tempted, he is able to help those who are tempted.*

Lord Jesus, your humility and heart of grace is something I just can't comprehend. You didn't hold on to your equality with the Father, but you made yourself nothing, taking on the very nature of a servant in human likeness.

You became like us in every way, with all our weakness and frailty so that you could stand before God as our merciful and faithful high priest.

You humbled yourself and became obedient to death, making atonement for our sins. You have freed me from the curse of sin and death.

You have given me freedom and liberty to live at peace with your Father. I worship you, my Lord and Saviour. I am so thankful to you for saving me, amen.

# Partners in a heavenly calling

## Hebrews 3:1-6

*Therefore, holy brothers, partakers of a heavenly calling, consider the Apostle and High Priest of our confession: Jesus, who was faithful to him who appointed him, as also Moses was in all his house.*

*For he has been counted worthy of more glory than Moses, because he who built the house has more honor than the house.*

*For every house is built by someone; but he who built all things is God. Moses indeed was faithful in all his house as a servant, for a testimony of those things which were afterward to be spoken, but Christ is faithful as a Son over his house.*

*We are his house, if we hold fast our confidence and the glorying of our hope firm to the end.*

Lord God, with every new word I read I am reminded of your faithfulness toward me. I pray that daily you will help me fix my thoughts on you.

Help me to remember your sacrifice at the cross, your humility and mercy extended towards your people. Help me to get up each morning determined to serve those around me.

I ask you give me a heart that looks to the good of others and is not centred around myself. I belong to you, and I ask that you form your character in me.

Help me to be compassionate and gracious, slow to anger and abounding in loving-kindness. I know that I lack so much in these areas.

Change me. Give me the grace and courage to live according to your word. Forgive me my many failings, especially my self-centred heart. I don't want this in my life. I want to reflect you. I ask in Jesus name, amen.

# Do not harden your hearts
## Hebrews 3:7-15

*Therefore, even as the Holy Spirit says,*

*"Today if you will hear his voice, don't harden your hearts, as in the rebellion, in the day of the trial in the wilderness, where your fathers tested me and tried me, and saw my deeds for forty years."*

*Therefore I was displeased with that generation, and said, "They always err in their heart, but they didn't know my ways." As I swore in my wrath, "They will not enter into my rest."*

*Beware, brothers, lest perhaps there might be in any one of you an evil heart of unbelief, in falling away from the living God; but exhort one another day*

*by day, so long as it is called 'today', lest*
*any one of you be hardened by the*
*deceitfulness of sin.*

*For we have become partakers of Christ,*
*if we hold the beginning of our*
*confidence firm to the end, while it is*
*said, "Today if you will hear his voice,*
*don't harden your hearts, as in the*
*rebellion."*

O God, forgive me for the times when I have heard your word, and did not obey. I want to love you with all my heart, mind, soul and strength. I want to take every word you speak and walk in obedience always.

Yet so often I find myself doing the things I set out not to do. I have the desire to do the right thing, but often when it comes down to it, I take the easy way out and do whatever I want.

I am so tired of this struggle. I'm so tired of failing you. I don't want to walk in disobedience and unbelief like so many of the Israelites did in the Old Testament.

I am reminded of the words of Paul when he said, "What a wretched man I am! Who will rescue me from this body of death? Thanks be to God – through Jesus Christ our Lord!

Therefore there is now no condemnation for those who are in Christ Jesus. I have been set free from the law of sin and death.

Thank you that I belong to you. Thank you that it is your work in me that changes me. Father, thank you for your forgiveness, and thank you that you have set your Spirit in me to lead me in your ways.

Thank you that I stand pure and clean before you and need have no fear, as my sins have been completely removed through the precious blood of Jesus. Thank you, amen.

# Warning against unbelief

## Hebrews 3:16-19

*For who, when they heard, rebelled?
Wasn't it all those who came out of Egypt
led by Moses?*

*With whom was he displeased forty
years?*

*Wasn't it with those who sinned, whose
bodies fell in the wilderness?*

*To whom did he swear that they wouldn't
enter into his rest, but to those who were
disobedient?*

*We see that they weren't able to enter in
because of unbelief.*

As I read these verses, I am reminded of my
unbelieving friends and family. Lord God, I pray you
would have mercy upon them. I ask that you reveal

yourself so they might come to a knowledge of the truth. Save them. Turn their hearts from wickedness to their need for a Saviour.

I ask you would give me opportunity to share what you have done, with them. Please Lord, open their hearts and minds to you that they might be saved. Give them eyes that see, and ears that hear. I ask in Jesus name, amen.

# Do not harden your hearts

## Hebrews 4:1-7

*Let's fear therefore, lest perhaps anyone of you should seem to have come short of a promise of entering into his rest.*

*For indeed we have had good news preached to us, even as they also did, but the word they heard didn't profit them, because it wasn't mixed with faith by those who heard.*

*For we who have believed do enter into that rest, even as he has said, "As I swore in my wrath, they will not enter into my rest;" although the works were finished from the foundation of the world.*

*For he has said this somewhere about the seventh day, "God rested on the seventh day from all his works;" and in this place again, "They will not enter into my rest."*

*Seeing therefore it remains that some should enter into it, and they to whom the good news was preached before failed to enter in because of disobedience, he again defines a certain day, today, saying through David so long a time afterward (just as has been said),*

*"Today if you will hear his voice, don't harden your hearts."*

Lord God, thank for giving me the gift of faith. I pray I might grow in faith as I read and obey your word. I want a humble heart. I want to submit myself to doing things your way.

I'm so sorry for the many times I have ignored the importance of the needs of my spirit.

As I read about the need to be careful not to fall short of entering your rest, I realise that I don't think much about my own walk with you. I don't 'examine or test myself' to see if I am in the faith. I am ashamed to admit that life's busyness often gets in the way.

Forgive me. I don't want to live like that. I want to grow in my relationship with you. I want to walk in obedience. I want to draw close to you and know you more. I want to continue in the rest you have given me.

Please help me in this, I ask in Jesus name, amen.

# Entering God's rest

## Hebrews 4:8-13

*For if Joshua had given them rest, he would not have spoken afterward of another day. There remains therefore a Sabbath rest for the people of God.*

*For he who has entered into his rest has himself also rested from his works, as God did from his.*

*Let's therefore give diligence to enter into that rest, lest anyone fall after the same example of disobedience.*

*For the word of God is living and active, and sharper than any two-edged sword, piercing even to the dividing of soul and spirit, of both joints and marrow, and is able to discern the thoughts and intentions of the heart.*

*There is no creature that is hidden from his sight, but all things are naked and laid open before the eyes of him to whom we must give an account.*

Thank you Lord for the Sabbath rest you give us. We don't need to work for our salvation. You, Lord Jesus have done it all.

Your shed blood purchased me and set me free from the snare of sin and a future in hell. I know it is your work alone that saves me. I know there is nothing I can contribute to what you have done.

All I can do is hold out my hands in gratitude for your loving mercy and goodness. Grant me a steadfast heart, and eyes that are fixed only on you.

Help me to persevere in faithfulness to your name even when things are tough. I pray that you would lead me away from temptation, but if it were to strike,

I pray that I might have the strength to overcome it. As I read, let your word become deeply embedded into my heart. For I know that your word will deal with every area of my life. Your word is living and active. It is life changing, and full of wisdom and love.

I want my thoughts and attitudes of heart to be searched by you. I ask that you expose any sinful attitude I might have. I don't want anything in my life that grieves you.

O God, you are the desire of my heart, and I love you. Amen.

# Confidently approaching the throne

## Hebrews 4:14-16

*Having then a great high priest who has passed through the heavens, Jesus, the Son of God, let's hold tightly to our confession.*

*For we don't have a high priest who can't be touched with the feeling of our infirmities, but one who has been in all points tempted like we are, yet without sin.*

*Let's therefore draw near with boldness to the throne of grace, that we may receive mercy and may find grace for help in time of need.*

Father, I don't understand myself at times. I know you are good. I know that I can approach you with confidence, but why is it that so often I choose to go my own way?

Why do I feel guilt and shame over things I know you have forgiven? I know that nothing is hidden from you.

I don't want anything in my life to be hidden from you, yet my heart sometimes seems to desire the opposite of what I know to be right.

Lord God, please break through this confusion. I want to draw near to you, to truly understand your mercy and grace, so my feelings match up with my faith.

I want my heart to only desire things that please you. I ask that you refresh and renew my innermost being through the washing of your precious word.

I trust that you are changing me. I trust that you are moulding and shaping me into your image. You are my Lord and my Redeemer. Amen.

# He was heard because of His devotion

## Hebrews 5:1-10

*For every high priest, being taken from among men, is appointed for men in things pertaining to God, that he may offer both gifts and sacrifices for sins.*

*The high priest can deal gently with those who are ignorant and going astray, because he himself is also surrounded with weakness. Because of this, he must offer sacrifices for sins for the people, as well as for himself.*

*Nobody takes this honor on himself, but he is called by God, just like Aaron was. So also Christ didn't glorify himself to be made a high priest, but it was he who said to him,*

*"You are my Son. Today I have become your father."*

*As he says also in another place,*

*"You are a priest forever, after the order of Melchizedek."*

*He, in the days of his flesh, having offered up prayers and petitions with strong crying and tears to him who was able to save him from death, and having been heard for his godly fear, though he was a Son, yet learned obedience by the things which he suffered.*

*Having been made perfect, he became to all of those who obey him the author of eternal salvation, named by God a high priest after the order of Melchizedek.*

Lord Jesus, teach me to pray. As I study your word I see how often you went aside and spent time with your Father.

You were steadfast always in following the Father's direction for your life. You trusted God implicitly, and without reservation.

I love the phrase, 'he was heard because of his devotion.' Not only that, but you learned obedience through suffering, and it was only through total obedience and humility that you were able to bring about God's perfect purpose.

Lord Jesus, the desire of my heart, from my innermost being, is to bring honour to your name. I want to learn complete obedience to you, in my thoughts, in my attitudes and in everything I do.

I want people to be drawn to you through the way I live my life. I want humility of heart and I will submit to anything you choose to bring about in my life. Only let it be for your glory. I ask in your most holy name, Jesus, amen.

# Milk... or solid food?

## Hebrews 5:11-14

*About him we have many words to say, and hard to interpret, seeing you have become dull of hearing.*

*For although by this time you should be teachers, you again need to have someone teach you the rudiments of the first principles of the revelations of God.*

*You have come to need milk, and not solid food. For everyone who lives on milk is not experienced in the word of righteousness, for he is a baby.*

*But solid food is for those who are full grown, who by reason of use have their senses exercised to discern good and evil.*

O God, your word is trustworthy and always right. It is the foundation on which I live my life. It sustains my heart and provides direction for every area of my life.

It is my refuge in time of trouble, and a stronghold through every storm. It lifts my heart when I am down, it brings wisdom when I don't know what to do, and it instructs me in righteousness. It brings me joy in drawing close to you.

I pray for my church. I ask that we will love your word with our whole heart.

I pray that we will grow in your word and in the knowledge of you, so we might be mature and complete not lacking anything.

I pray we will not be content to chew on elementary truths, loving milk, instead of wanting to grow and eat solid food.

I pray that our hearts might be inclined towards study and searching for truth, always seeking to know you more. In Jesus name I pray, amen.

# Progress beyond elementary instructions

## Hebrews 6:1-3

*Therefore leaving the teaching of the first principles of Christ, let's press on to perfection—not laying again a foundation of repentance from dead works, of faith toward God, of the teaching of baptisms, of laying on of hands, of resurrection of the dead, and of eternal judgment. This will we do, if God permits.*

Lord God, I don't want to be a Christian settled in 'elementary instructions.' I want to know them well, but I want to grow in faith. I want grow in love and knowledge of you, and I know that it will take effort and study. But I want to do it.

Please help me to want to.  I want your word to dwell in me richly, so that I might know Christ and the power of His resurrection. I want my life to be saturated with your Word so I might know you more.

I want to walk according to your ways, even if it involves suffering and trials.  Help me to have a steadfast mindset.  Show me your ways, O God, and lead me in the way of everlasting life.  I ask in Jesus name, amen.

# Don't be sluggish!
## Hebrew 6:4-12

*For concerning those who were once enlightened and tasted of the heavenly gift, and were made partakers of the Holy Spirit, and tasted the good word of God and the powers of the age to come, and then fell away, it is impossible to renew them again to repentance; seeing they crucify the Son of God for themselves again, and put him to open shame.*

*For the land which has drunk the rain that comes often on it and produces a crop suitable for them for whose sake it is also tilled, receives blessing from God; but if it bears thorns and thistles, it is rejected and near being cursed, whose end is to be burned.*

37

*But, beloved, we are persuaded of better things for you, and things that accompany salvation, even though we speak like this.*

*For God is not unrighteous, so as to forget your work and the labor of love which you showed toward his name, in that you served the saints, and still do serve them.*

*We desire that each one of you may show the same diligence to the fullness of hope even to the end, that you won't be sluggish, but imitators of those who through faith and perseverance inherited the promises.*

Father, I ask that you deliver me from evil. I ask that you will give me grace and strength in times of testing, so that instead of falling away, I will continue to be strengthened in faith.

Lord, as I read this passage, I ask you will protect me from ever falling away from you. My heart trembles at the thought of living without you.

I can't imagine what purpose there is in living a life without your guidance and instruction.

Lord I want more of you. Renew my mind, and refresh my soul with the beauty of your word. Forgive my sins, in Jesus name, amen.

# The hope set before us

## Hebrews 6:13-20

*For when God made a promise to Abraham, since he could swear by no one greater, he swore by himself, saying,*

*"Surely blessing I will bless you, and multiplying I will multiply you."*

*Thus, having patiently endured, he obtained the promise. For men indeed swear by a greater one, and in every dispute of theirs the oath is final for confirmation.*

*In this way God, being determined to show more abundantly to the heirs of the promise the immutability of his counsel, interposed with an oath, that by two immutable things, in which it is*

40

*impossible for God to lie, we may have a strong encouragement, who have fled for refuge to take hold of the hope set before us.*

*This hope we have as an anchor of the soul, a hope both sure and steadfast and entering into that which is within the veil; where as a forerunner Jesus entered for us, having become a high priest forever after the order of Melchizedek.*

When reading this passage I am reminded of the beautiful hymn by Stuart K Hine. The words make a wonderful prayer.

O Lord, my God, when I in awesome wonder
Consider all the worlds Thy Hands have made;
I see the stars, I hear the rolling thunder,
Thy power throughout the universe displayed

Then sings my soul, My Saviour God, to Thee,
How great Thou art, how great Thou art.
Then sings my soul, My Saviour God, to Thee,
How great Thou art, how great Thou art!

And when I think of God, His Son not sparing;
Sent Him to die, I scarce can take it in;
That on the Cross, my burden gladly bearing,
He bled and died to take away my sin.

When Christ shall come with shout of acclamation
And lead me home, what joy shall fill my heart!
Then I shall bow with humble adoration,
And then proclaim, 'My God, how great Thou art!'

Then sings my soul, My Saviour God, to Thee,
How great Thou art, how great Thou art.
Then sings my soul, My Saviour God, to Thee,
How great Thou art, how great Thou art

You are the anchor for my soul, the encouragement and lifter of my heart. Amen.

# Abraham honours Melchizedek

## Hebrews 7:1-10

*For this Melchizedek, king of Salem, priest of God Most High, who met Abraham returning from the slaughter of the kings and blessed him, to whom also Abraham divided a tenth part of all (being first, by interpretation, "king of righteousness", and then also "king of Salem", which means "king of peace," without father, without mother, without genealogy, having neither beginning of days nor end of life, but made like the Son of God), remains a priest continually.*

*Now consider how great this man was, to whom even Abraham, the patriarch, gave a tenth out of the best plunder.*

*They indeed of the sons of Levi who
receive the priest's office have a
commandment to take tithes of the people
according to the law, that is, of their
brothers, though these have come out of
the body of Abraham, but he whose
genealogy is not counted from them has
accepted tithes from Abraham, and has
blessed him who has the promises.*

*But without any dispute the lesser is
blessed by the greater.*

*Here people who die receive tithes, but
there one receives tithes of whom it is
testified that he lives.*

*We can say that through Abraham even
Levi, who receives tithes, has paid tithes,
for he was yet in the body of his father
when Melchizedek met him.*

Father, as I read this passage and see Abraham giving
Melchisedek a tithe of what he had received, I am
reminded of the passage where Paul urges the
Romans to offer their bodies as living sacrifices.

He said it was their reasonable act of worship. It was
reasonable of Abraham to give Melchisedek a tenth
of the plunder, and it is reasonable for me, in the light

of your perfect mercy, to offer my whole self to you. Spirit, mind, soul and body.

Lord God, the desire of my heart is to please you. I pray you will give me strength not to conform to the pattern of this world. Your word is my foundation, and I know that all my thinking and perspective on living each day is influenced by reading my Bible.

O God, take me and mould me into the image of your Son. I belong to you. Do with me as you will, in Jesus name I pray, amen.

# The power of an indestructible life

## Hebrews 7:11-18

*Now if perfection was through the Levitical priesthood (for under it the people have received the law), what further need was there for another priest to arise after the order of Melchizedek, and not be called after the order of Aaron?*

*For the priesthood being changed, there is of necessity a change made also in the law.*

*For he of whom these things are said belongs to another tribe, from which no one has officiated at the altar.*

*For it is evident that our Lord has sprung out of Judah, about which tribe Moses spoke nothing concerning priesthood.*

*This is yet more abundantly evident, if after the likeness of Melchizedek there arises another priest, who has been made, not after the law of a fleshly commandment, but after the power of an endless life; for it is testified,*

*"You are a priest forever, according to the order of Melchizedek."*

*For there is an annulling of a foregoing commandment because of its weakness and uselessness (for the law made nothing perfect)...*

Lord God, it is by your grace I have been saved, not by any effort of my own, but received as a precious gift from a loving Father. Jesus perfect sacrifice is enough. There is nothing I can add to it.

By your grace I have received beautiful promises whereby I need never fear want, or direction, or protection. You provide my every need.

You provide a way for me to walk, and you are a shield to me against the fiery darts of the evil one. All of this you have provided through your Son Jesus.

Lord Jesus, you are my true hope by whom I draw near to God. You are my Saviour, my Lord, my King. You are my Wonderful Counsellor, Mighty God, Everlasting Father, and Prince of Peace. You rule and reign forever. Amen.

# Jesus, our guarantee...

## Hebrews 7:19-28

*...and a bringing in of a better hope, through which we draw near to God. Inasmuch as he was not made priest without the taking of an oath (for they indeed have been made priests without an oath), but he with an oath by him that says of him,*

*"The Lord swore and will not change his mind, 'You are a priest forever, according to the order of Melchizedek.'"*

*By so much, Jesus has become the collateral of a better covenant. Many, indeed, have been made priests, because they are hindered from continuing by death. But he, because he lives forever, has his priesthood unchangeable.*

*Therefore he is also able to save to the uttermost those who draw near to God through him, seeing that he lives forever to make intercession for them.*

*For such a high priest was fitting for us: holy, guiltless, undefiled, separated from sinners, and made higher than the heavens; who doesn't need, like those high priests, to offer up sacrifices daily, first for his own sins, and then for the sins of the people.*

*For he did this once for all, when he offered up himself. For the law appoints men as high priests who have weakness, but the word of the oath which came after the law appoints a Son forever who has been perfected.*

Lord Jesus, you are our great high priest. You became the ultimate sacrifice and now you sit at the right hand of God the Father, in glory and splendour.

Your sacrifice does not have to be done over and over again, your sacrifice stands forever. You are from everlasting to everlasting, and you reign over all.

You have chosen a people for yourself and made them holy through the washing of your blood. Your death tore the temple veil in two, from top to bottom.

There was no shred of a barrier left to stop man enjoying a relationship with God.

Lord Jesus, you loved the church and gave yourself up for us, cleansing us and presenting us to yourself as a radiant church without stain or wrinkle, but holy and blameless. Lord, I am so grateful that you have made me yours. Amen.

# We have such a high priest
## Hebrews 8:1-6

*Now in the things which we are saying, the main point is this. We have such a high priest, who sat down on the right hand of the throne of the Majesty in the heavens, a servant of the sanctuary and of the true tabernacle, which the Lord pitched, not man.*

*For every high priest is appointed to offer both gifts and sacrifices. Therefore it is necessary that this high priest also have something to offer.*

*For if he were on earth, he would not be a priest at all, seeing there are priests who offer the gifts according to the law, who serve a copy and shadow of the heavenly things, even as Moses was*

*warned by God when he was about to*
*make the tabernacle, for he said,*

*"See, you shall make everything*
*according to the pattern that was shown*
*to you on the mountain."*

*But now he has obtained a more*
*excellent ministry, by so much as he is*
*also the mediator of a better covenant,*
*which on better promises has been given*
*as law.*

Lord Jesus, thank you that we no longer need to bring sacrifices, and to go to a single place to worship every year, but instead you are our High Priest.

You intercede for your people day and night before the throne of grace. You never fail. You never grow weary. You always do the will of the Father.

Whilst you are now our mediator and the pattern of the tabernacle and temple is done away with, I am so grateful for the wisdom of the Old Testament.

Thank you, Father, that you caused your words to be written down, so that generation upon generations of people might be blessed. Thank you for revealing human weakness, and thank you for revealing your holy grace.

Thank you for the record of your determination to save your people. You bless obedience. You rebuke in order to restore.

Holy is your name. I want to live my life according to the pattern given in your word. Help me to be obedient and not stray from what is written. In Jesus name I pray, amen.

# And I will be their God

## Hebrews 8:7-13

*For if that first covenant had been faultless, then no place would have been sought for a second. For finding fault with them, he said,*

*"Behold, the days come", says the Lord, "that I will make a new covenant with the house of Israel and with the house of Judah; not according to the covenant that I made with their fathers, in the day that I took them by the hand to lead them out of the land of Egypt; for they didn't continue in my covenant, and I disregarded them," says the Lord.*

*"For this is the covenant that I will make with the house of Israel. After those days," says the Lord; "I will put my laws*

*into their mind, I will also write them on their heart.*

*I will be their God, and they will be my people.*

*They will not teach every man his fellow citizen, and every man his brother, saying, 'Know the Lord,' for all will know me, from their least to their greatest.*

*For I will be merciful to their unrighteousness. I will remember their sins and lawless deeds no more."*

*In that he says, "A new covenant", he has made the first old. But that which is becoming old and grows aged is near to vanishing away.*

Father, thank you for your wisdom in showing us that we cannot keep your laws by ourselves. It is impossible to please you by 'trying.' The Israelites tried, and constantly failed. They were forever being drawn away from you by the sin of the surrounding nations.

I know that I am just like them. I know that if I don't look to you always, I will look to something else, and be drawn away from you by sin. Thank you for the new covenant. Thank you that the old is done away with and the new is now established.

Lord Jesus, you now sit at the right hand of the throne of the Majesty in heaven. You have put your Spirit in our hearts so that we can cry, Abba, Father. You have put your laws in our minds, and written them on our hearts.

You are our God, and we are your people. Our sin has been removed as far as the East is from the West.

Because of your beloved Son, my sin is remembered no more. I stand before you, and am declared not guilty. What amazing grace! Blessed be your holy name. Amen.

# The way to God was not yet open

## Hebrews 9:1-10

*Now indeed even the first covenant had ordinances of divine service and an earthly sanctuary. For a tabernacle was prepared. In the first part were the lamp stand, the table, and the show bread; which is called the Holy Place.*

*After the second veil was the tabernacle which is called the Holy of Holies, having a golden altar of incense, and the ark of the covenant overlaid on all sides with gold, in which was a golden pot holding the manna, Aaron's rod that budded, and the tablets of the covenant; and above it cherubim of glory*

*overshadowing the mercy seat, of which
things we can't speak now in detail.*

*Now these things having been thus
prepared, the priests go in continually
into the first tabernacle, accomplishing
the services, but into the second the high
priest alone, once in the year, not without
blood, which he offers for himself, and
for the errors of the people.*

*The Holy Spirit is indicating this, that the
way into the Holy Place wasn't yet
revealed while the first tabernacle was
still standing.*

*This is a symbol of the present age,
where gifts and sacrifices are offered that
are incapable, concerning the
conscience, of making the worshiper
perfect, being only (with meats and
drinks and various washings) fleshly
ordinances, imposed until a time of
reformation.*

Father, as I read this passage I see how you taught the
Israelites that you need to be at the centre of
everything.

It reminds me that I should not come before you carelessly, but instead with a humble attitude of heart crying, 'hallowed be your name.'

It reminds me that always, the cross needs to be the centre of my thinking. The blood of Jesus is the reason I can come before you. The blood of Jesus has made me righteous in your sight.

It has washed away my sin and speaks of the vastness of your love for us. Thank you. I am so grateful for your saving work in my life.

Forgive me the many times when I have not remembered to put you first. Forgive me for the times I have taken you for granted.

I pray you will create in me a humble and contrite heart. I want to worship you in Spirit and in truth, always with reverence and awe. You are holy, and you alone are worthy of honour and praise. Amen.

# The blood of Christ
## Hebrews 9:11-22

*But Christ having come as a high priest
of the coming good things, through the
greater and more perfect tabernacle, not
made with hands, that is to say, not of
this creation, nor yet through the blood
of goats and calves, but through his own
blood, entered in once for all into the
Holy Place, having obtained eternal
redemption.*

*For if the blood of goats and bulls, and
the ashes of a heifer sprinkling those who
have been defiled, sanctify to the
cleanness of the flesh, how much more
will the blood of Christ, who through the
eternal Spirit offered himself without
defect to God, cleanse your conscience
from dead works to serve the living God?*

*For this reason he is the mediator of a new covenant, since a death has occurred for the redemption of the transgressions that were under the first covenant, that those who have been called may receive the promise of the eternal inheritance.*

*For where a last will and testament is, there must of necessity be the death of him who made it. For a will is in force where there has been death, for it is never in force while he who made it lives.*

*Therefore even the first covenant has not been dedicated without blood. For when every commandment had been spoken by Moses to all the people according to the law, he took the blood of the calves and the goats, with water and scarlet wool and hyssop, and sprinkled both the book itself and all the people, saying,*

*"This is the blood of the covenant which God has commanded you."*

*Moreover he sprinkled the tabernacle and all the vessels of the ministry in the same way with the blood.*

*According to the law, nearly everything is cleansed with blood, and apart from shedding of blood there is no remission.*

Lord Jesus, thank you for your sacrifice on the cross. Thank you that you have set me free from the power of sin.

You have cleansed my conscience so that I might not be consumed by guilt. I stand before your throne, sure in the knowledge that my sins have been dealt with.

Words cannot express how very grateful I am. Thank you for the surety of my future. Your word promises us an inheritance and I really have no idea what that could mean!

I know it will be beyond anything we can possibly imagine. I find myself longing for the day when I can see you face to face. What a wonderful day that will be!

Your word speaks of joining the angels in worship, seeing your glory, ruling and reigning, receiving a crown, receiving a reward.

My heart sings for joy for such an unspeakably incredible future. All praise and honour and glory and power to Him who sits on the throne and to the Lamb, for ever and ever! Amen!

# Jesus bore the sins of many

## Hebrews 9:23-28

*It was necessary therefore that the copies of the things in the heavens should be cleansed with these, but the heavenly things themselves with better sacrifices than these.*

*For Christ hasn't entered into holy places made with hands, which are representations of the true, but into heaven itself, now to appear in the presence of God for us; nor yet that he should offer himself often, as the high priest enters into the holy place year by year with blood not his own, or else he must have suffered often since the foundation of the world.*

*But now once at the end of the ages, he
has been revealed to put away sin by the
sacrifice of himself.*

*Inasmuch as it is appointed for men to
die once, and after this, judgment, so
Christ also, having been offered once to
bear the sins of many, will appear a
second time, without sin, to those who
are eagerly waiting for him for salvation.*

Lord Jesus, your sacrifice took away the sins of many people. Your word says that your sheep listen to your voice, you know them and they follow you.

You have promised them eternal life and that no-one can snatch them out of your hand. Your Father has given them to you. How wonderful to know that I have been given to you by the Father.

Lord God, you rescued me from the dominion of darkness, and brought me into the kingdom of your Son whom you love.

When I was dead in sin, you breathed your Spirit into me and gave me life. I have been redeemed and all my sins forgiven. You bring salvation to all who wait for you. Blessed be your holy name, amen.

# Impossible for the blood of bulls and goats to take away sins

## Hebrews 10:1-7

*For the law, having a shadow of the good to come, not the very image of the things, can never with the same sacrifices year by year, which they offer continually, make perfect those who draw near.*

*Or else wouldn't they have ceased to be offered, because the worshipers, having been once cleansed, would have had no more consciousness of sins?*

*But in those sacrifices there is a yearly reminder of sins. For it is impossible that the blood of bulls and goats should take away sins. Therefore when he comes into the world, he says,*

*"You didn't desire sacrifice and offering, but you prepared a body for me. You had no pleasure in whole burnt offerings and sacrifices for sin. Then I said, 'Behold, I*

*have come (in the scroll of the book it is written of me) to do your will, O God.'"*

Lord Jesus, you came to earth to do the will of the Father. All through your life you told us that 'you came from heaven to do the will of Him who sent me, not my own will.

You said, 'my food is to do the will of Him who sent me and to finish His work. And you said, 'not my will, but yours be done,' in Gethsemane.

You poured out your life here on earth showing us how to live, and what to live for. This is what I want. I want to do the will of the Father, not my own will.

I want your will to be as food to me. Essential and always needed. I want you to be glorified in my life, not myself. I love to serve you and find such joy in obeying your word.

You are my King, my Lord, my God. Whom else is there worthy to give my life to? There is no-one else! I want to do your will.

Give me grace to complete the work you have set before me, in Jesus name I pray, amen.

# I have come to do your will

## Hebrews 10:8-18

*Previously saying, "Sacrifices and offerings and whole burnt offerings and sacrifices for sin you didn't desire, neither had pleasure in them" (those which are offered according to the law), then he has said, "Behold, I have come to do your will."*

*He takes away the first, that he may establish the second, by which will we have been sanctified through the offering of the body of Jesus Christ once for all.*

*Every priest indeed stands day by day serving and offering often the same sacrifices which can never take away sins, but he, when he had offered one sacrifice for sins forever, sat down on the*

*right hand of God, from that time waiting*
*until his enemies are made the footstool*
*of his feet.*

*For by one offering he has perfected*
*forever those who are being sanctified.*
*The Holy Spirit also testifies to us, for*
*after saying,*

*"This is the covenant that I will make*
*with them: 'After those days,' says the*
*Lord, 'I will put my laws on their heart, I*
*will also write them on their mind;'"*

*then he says,*

*"I will remember their sins and their*
*iniquities no more."*

*Now where remission of these is, there is*
*no more offering for sin.*

Who among the gods is like you, O Lord? Who is like you – majestic in holiness, awesome in glory, working wonders?

You spoke and creation came into being. Your unfailing love leads the people you have redeemed. In your strength you guide them in your paths, and by your grace you lead them to a home more beautiful than any can imagine.

By your sacrifice you have made your people perfect forever, each one of us being made holy. You have set your law upon our hearts, and our minds are filled with your word.

You guide us in paths of righteousness for your name's sake. Our sins and lawless acts you remember no more.

Oh God, my God! What mercy and grace you have extended to us! Who can fathom the depths of your love? What words are there that can properly express our gratitude? God of holiness. God of glory. God of wonders. How great is your name!

# Let us draw near

## Hebrews 10:19-25

*Having therefore, brothers, boldness to enter into the holy place by the blood of Jesus, by the way which he dedicated for us, a new and living way, through the veil, that is to say, his flesh, and having a great priest over God's house, let's draw near with a true heart in fullness of faith, having our hearts sprinkled from an evil conscience, and having our body washed with pure water, let's hold fast the confession of our hope without wavering; for he who promised is faithful.*

*Let's consider how to provoke one another to love and good works, not forsaking our own assembling together, as the custom of some is, but exhorting*

*one another, and so much the more as*
*you see the Day approaching.*

Lord Jesus, when you died, the veil of the temple was torn in two, and for the first time since the Garden of Eden, man could come into the presence of God.

Thank you that you have taken away my guilt. You have cleansed me and removed my sin completely. You have made me pure so that I might approach the Father without fear.

As I read this passage of scripture, I want with all my heart to do your will. I want to be unswerving in my faith. I want always the hope you have given me to govern my life. And I want to encourage others towards love and good deeds. I want to be an encouragement wherever I go.

My life belongs to you. Form your character in me, I pray. Change my heart, so that my desires might line up with what you desire. Change my mind, so that I might act in kindness and love.

Rebuke me and discipline me when needed. Cause every wrong attitude to be brought to the light so I can repent of it. I want only you, my Lord and my God. I ask all this in your holy name, Jesus, amen.

# Obedient and holy lives

## Hebrews 10:26-39

*For if we sin wilfully after we have received the knowledge of the truth, there remains no more a sacrifice for sins, but a certain fearful expectation of judgment, and a fierceness of fire which will devour the adversaries.*

*A man who disregards Moses' law dies without compassion on the word of two or three witnesses. How much worse punishment do you think he will be judged worthy of who has trodden under foot the Son of God, and has counted the blood of the covenant with which he was sanctified an unholy thing, and has insulted the Spirit of grace?*

*For we know him who said, "Vengeance belongs to me. I will repay," says the Lord. Again, "The Lord will judge his people." It is a fearful thing to fall into the hands of the living God.*

*But remember the former days, in which, after you were enlightened, you endured a great struggle with sufferings; partly, being exposed to both reproaches and oppressions; and partly, becoming partakers with those who were treated so.*

*For you both had compassion on me in my chains, and joyfully accepted the plundering of your possessions, knowing that you have for yourselves a better possession and an enduring one in the heavens.*

*Therefore don't throw away your boldness, which has a great reward. For you need endurance so that, having done the will of God, you may receive the promise.*

*"In a very little while, he who comes will come, and will not wait. But the righteous will live by faith. If he shrinks back, my soul has no pleasure in him."*

74

*But we are not of those who shrink back*
*to destruction, but of those who have*
*faith to the saving of the soul.*

Lord God, I pray you will keep my heart soft, and my ears open. I pray that I will always want to listen and obey. Let me never fall into the trap of thinking my desires are more important than your ways.

I pray for my church. I ask that we might be faithful towards each other, and towards you. I pray you will fill us with your Spirit. Give us hunger for your word, and a constant desire to do the works you put in front of us to do.

I pray for my neighbours, and family, and friends, who are in danger of judgement and raging fire. I ask for mercy, and that you would stretch out your hand and save them.

My heart is heavy at the thought of them suffering eternal punishment. Lord, for the sake of your name, bring them into your kingdom. Work upon their lives so that they might come to you.

Glorify yourself through them, and fill your church with new believers. I pray that we might live by faith, never shrinking back, but always looking forward. Always taking hold of your word and walking in your light. I ask this in Jesus name, amen.

# Faith – being sure of our hope
## Hebrews 11:1-6

*Now faith is assurance of things hoped for, proof of things not seen. For by this, the elders obtained testimony. By faith, we understand that the universe has been framed by the word of God, so that what is seen has not been made out of things which are visible.*

*By faith, Abel offered to God a more excellent sacrifice than Cain, through which he had testimony given to him that he was righteous, God testifying with respect to his gifts; and through it he, being dead, still speaks.*

*By faith, Enoch was taken away, so that he wouldn't see death, and he was not found, because God translated him. For*

*he has had testimony given to him that*
*before his translation he had been well*
*pleasing to God. Without faith it is*
*impossible to be well pleasing to him, for*
*he who comes to God must believe that*
*he exists, and that he is a rewarder of*
*those who seek him.*

O Holy God, you are the eternal One. You see into men's hearts and see what is really there. Lord, I pray that you will change my heart.

I pray I will learn daily to walk by faith and not by sight. I pray that I will always remember that you will do more than I could ever ask or imagine.

I want my trust in you to be absolute. I want no doubt to be found in my heart. O God, give me eyes that see, and ears that hear your word. Grant that I might grow daily in faith.

I pray you will give me grace to earnestly seek you each day. More than anything, I want to please you. In Jesus name I ask, amen.

# By faith, Noah...

## Hebrews 11:7-16

*By faith, Noah, being warned about things not yet seen, moved with godly fear, prepared a ship for the saving of his house, through which he condemned the world, and became heir of the righteousness which is according to faith.*

*By faith, Abraham, when he was called, obeyed to go out to the place which he was to receive for an inheritance. He went out, not knowing where he went.*

*By faith, he lived as an alien in the land of promise, as in a land not his own, dwelling in tents with Isaac and Jacob, the heirs with him of the same promise.*

*For he looked for the city which has the foundations, whose builder and maker is God.*

*By faith, even Sarah herself received power to conceive, and she bore a child when she was past age, since she counted him faithful who had promised.*

*Therefore as many as the stars of the sky in multitude, and as innumerable as the sand which is by the sea shore, were fathered by one man, and him as good as dead.*

*These all died in faith, not having received the promises, but having seen them and embraced them from afar, and having confessed that they were strangers and pilgrims on the earth.*

*For those who say such things make it clear that they are seeking a country of their own. If indeed they had been thinking of that country from which they went out, they would have had enough time to return.*

*But now they desire a better country, that is, a heavenly one. Therefore God is not ashamed of them, to be called their God, for he has prepared a city for them.*

Lord, as I read your word, I see how these men heard from you, and lived their lives according to what you spoke and promised them.

They lived knowing they could trust you, and were completely sure that everything you told them would come to pass.

Father, I am ashamed of the unbelief in my life. I am not content to live one day in faith and the next in doubt. I do not want to be double-minded. I pray as I read your word that I will grow in faith. I want to be different tomorrow than I am today.

I want to see you. I want to know you more. Father, help overcome my lack of faith. I ask in Jesus name, amen.

# By faith, Abraham...
## Hebrews 11:17-31

*By faith, Abraham, being tested, offered up Isaac. Yes, he who had gladly received the promises was offering up his one and only son, to whom it was said, "Your offspring will be accounted as from Isaac," concluding that God is able to raise up even from the dead.*

*Figuratively speaking, he also did receive him back from the dead.*

*By faith, Isaac blessed Jacob and Esau, even concerning things to come.*

*By faith, Jacob, when he was dying, blessed each of the sons of Joseph, and worshiped, leaning on the top of his staff.*

*By faith, Joseph, when his end was near, made mention of the departure of the children of Israel, and gave instructions concerning his bones.*

*By faith, Moses, when he was born, was hidden for three months by his parents, because they saw that he was a beautiful child, and they were not afraid of the king's commandment.*

*By faith, Moses, when he had grown up, refused to be called the son of Pharaoh's daughter, choosing rather to share ill treatment with God's people than to enjoy the pleasures of sin for a time, considering the reproach of Christ greater riches than the treasures of Egypt; for he looked to the reward.*

*By faith, he left Egypt, not fearing the wrath of the king; for he endured, as seeing him who is invisible.*

*By faith, he kept the Passover, and the sprinkling of the blood, that the destroyer of the firstborn should not touch them.*

*By faith, they passed through the Red Sea as on dry land. When the Egyptians tried to do so, they were swallowed up. By*

*faith, the walls of Jericho fell down, after*
*they had been encircled for seven days.*

*By faith, Rahab the prostitute didn't*
*perish with those who were disobedient,*
*having received the spies in peace.*

Father, I want the kind of faith these ancient believers had.  I want that kind of courage and determination to follow you no matter the consequences.  None were perfect, but each came to trust whole-heartedly in you.

Grant me the faith to overcome my fear of what others think of me, and my fear of being different, and noticed, and rejected.  Form in me a steadfastness of character and integrity.

O God, I look to you.  My future is in your hands, and I know it is wonderful!  I love you Lord.  Amen.

# Commended for their faith

## Hebrews 11:32-40

*What more shall I say?*

*For the time would fail me if I told of
Gideon, Barak, Samson, Jephthah,
David, Samuel, and the prophets, who
through faith subdued kingdoms, worked
out righteousness, obtained promises,
stopped the mouths of lions, quenched
the power of fire, escaped the edge of the
sword, from weakness were made strong,
grew mighty in war, and caused foreign
armies to flee.*

*Women received their dead by
resurrection.*

*Others were tortured, not accepting their deliverance, that they might obtain a better resurrection.*

*Others were tried by mocking and scourging, yes, moreover by bonds and imprisonment. They were stoned. They were sawn apart.*

*They were tempted. They were slain with the sword.*

*They went around in sheep skins and in goat skins; being destitute, afflicted, ill-treated of whom the world was not worthy - wandering in deserts, mountains, caves, and the holes of the earth.*

*These all, having had testimony given to them through their faith, didn't receive the promise, God having provided some better thing concerning us, so that apart from us they should not be made perfect.*

Lord, you are the great life changer. You create new hearts, and you mould new characters. I thank you for each and every hardship you have put in my life. Thank you for using them to mould me, and discipline me, into the image of your beloved Son, my Lord and Saviour.

You gave me life when I was dead in sin. You gave me your Spirit, to lead me into righteousness. You gave me faith, that I might grow in trust and knowledge of you. Thank you for your precious word and promises. Amen.

# Run with endurance

## Hebrews 12:1-2

*Therefore let's also, seeing we are surrounded by so great a cloud of witnesses, lay aside every weight and the sin which so easily entangles us, and let's run with perseverance the race that is set before us, looking to Jesus, the author and perfecter of faith, who for the joy that was set before him endured the cross, despising its shame, and has sat down at the right hand of the throne of God.*

Lord God, thank you that I can look at the lives of believers who have gone before me. I can be encouraged and built up by their example. I can learn from their mistakes.

87

More than anything, I can learn how to draw close to you. Lord help me to walk away from petty sins and to keep my eyes firmly fixed on the cross of Christ.

When I look at the lives of the saints, one thing I see is the futility, and meaningless of life lived without you. Let me never forget this. Your word teaches that I am only a stranger in this world, and that the world to come, is my true home.

I ask you will instil in my heart true joy at this hope you have set before me. I know that my future with you, will contain more than I could ever ask or imagine.

Lord Jesus, let me be a part of lifting up your name in all the earth. Give me grace and courage to speak out of what you have done. In your name I ask, amen.

# Think of Him who endured such opposition
## Hebrews 12:3-6

*For consider him who has endured such contradiction of sinners against himself, that you don't grow weary, fainting in your souls.*

*You have not yet resisted to blood, striving against sin. You have forgotten the exhortation which reasons with you as with children,*

*"My son, don't take lightly the chastening of the Lord, nor faint when you are reproved by him; for whom the Lord loves, he disciplines, and chastises every son whom he receives."*

Father, I pray that I will not lose heart in my faithfulness to you. Give me always a thirst for your word so I might never turn away.

I pray that in my struggle against sin you will continue to give me grace to overcome; and in time of hardship and discipline, I might respond with humility and repentance. O Lord, let pride and arrogance have no part in my life.

I read of Moses, and how he faithfully looked to you and served the your people. So many times when things were difficult they turned against him and threatened him. But he was steadfast in bringing your word to them, loving and serving them. I want this kind of heart.

I don't want to give up or run away when things get difficult. I want to be faithful in speaking your word, whenever you give opportunity.

Give me a humble, faithful heart like Moses. I ask this in Jesus name, amen.

# Endure suffering as discipline
## Hebrews 12:7-13

*It is for discipline that you endure. God deals with you as with children, for what son is there whom his father doesn't discipline? But if you are without discipline, of which all have been made partakers, then you are illegitimate, and not children. Furthermore, we had the fathers of our flesh to chasten us, and we paid them respect. Shall we not much rather be in subjection to the Father of spirits, and live?*

*For they indeed, for a few days, punished us as seemed good to them; but he for our profit, that we may be partakers of his holiness. All chastening seems for the present to be not joyous but grievous; yet afterward it yields the peaceful fruit of righteousness to those who have been trained by it.*

*Therefore lift up the hands that hang down and the feeble knees, and make straight paths for your feet, so what is lame may not be dislocated, but rather be healed.*

Lord God, I welcome your discipline in my life. I welcome your work to train, correct, rebuke and mould me. Let me never lose sight of your love for me in these times. I want your work in me to produce a harvest of righteousness and peace, for your praise and your glory alone.

I read in the Old Testament how Israel was constantly led astray by their evil desires, but by your faithful discipline you brought them back to faith in you. I know myself to be just like them.

Thank you for your faithfulness toward those whom you love. Thank you that as your child I know that you will never let me go. You will never let me stray so far that I am lost. You discipline me and draw me back to you because of your great love.

Who is there like you O God? Glory be to your holy name! Amen.

# Pursue peace and holiness

## Hebrews 12:14-24

*Follow after peace with all men, and the
sanctification without which no man will
see the Lord, looking carefully lest there
be any man who falls short of the grace
of God, lest any root of bitterness
springing up trouble you, and many be
defiled by it, lest there be any sexually
immoral person, or profane person, like
Esau, who sold his birthright for one
meal.*

*For you know that even when he
afterward desired to inherit the blessing,
he was rejected, for he found no place
for a change of mind though he sought it
diligently with tears.*

*For you have not come to a mountain that might be touched, and that burned with fire, and to blackness, darkness, storm, the sound of a trumpet, and the voice of words; which those who heard it begged that not one more word should be spoken to them, for they could not stand that which was commanded,*

*"If even an animal touches the mountain, it shall be stoned."*

*So fearful was the appearance that Moses said, "I am terrified and trembling."*

*But you have come to Mount Zion, and to the city of the living God, the heavenly Jerusalem, and to innumerable multitudes of angels, to the festal gathering and assembly of the firstborn who are enrolled in heaven, to God the Judge of all, to the spirits of just men made perfect, to Jesus, the mediator of a new covenant, and to the blood of sprinkling that speaks better than that of Abel.*

Praise be to the God and Father of our Lord Jesus Christ, who alone does marvellous deeds! Praise be to His glorious name forever; may the whole earth be filled with His glory!

You lifted me up from the pit. When I was dead in sin, you gave me life. You lifted me up in heavenly places in Christ Jesus, where thousands upon thousands of angels meet in joyful assembly.

You brought me into your family the church, where your Son Jesus, rules forever. And you have made me righteous and perfect in your sight, forever. What amazing grace! What perfect love!

O God, in the light of all this, I want to live a life that brings honour to you. I ask that you mould my heart so that I might live in peace will all those around me. Grant me humility and wisdom, in Jesus name, amen.

# Let us give thanks

## Hebrews 12:25-29

*See that you don't refuse him who speaks.
For if they didn't escape when they
refused him who warned on the earth,
how much more will we not escape who
turn away from him who warns from
heaven, whose voice shook the earth
then, but now he has promised, saying,*

*"Yet once more I will shake not only the
earth, but also the heavens." This phrase,
"Yet once more" signifies the removing of
those things that are shaken, as of things
that have been made, that those things
which are not shaken may remain.*

*Therefore, receiving a Kingdom that
can't be shaken, let's have grace, through
which we serve God acceptably, with*

*reverence and awe, for our God is a*
*consuming fire.*

O God, you are a consuming fire. Your holiness and justice, your love and grace, are unfathomable.

O that I might know you more. Reveal your love to me. Show me your face that I might worship you in spirit and in truth. O Lord my God, how majestic is your name in all the earth!

I look forward to the day when you come and make all things new. You will sweep away evil and sin, and renew all things. The heart of every man will be laid bare and your perfect justice will be made known to all. Every knee will bow, and every tongue confess that Jesus Christ is Lord.

O God, I thank you for the living hope you have given me through this new birth. You have set before me an inheritance that can never perish, spoil or fade, kept in heaven for me.

Glory be to the Father, and to the Son and to the Holy Spirit, amen!

# Brotherly love must continue
## Hebrews 13:1-6

*Let brotherly love continue. Don't forget to show hospitality to strangers, for in doing so, some have entertained angels without knowing it.*

*Remember those who are in bonds, as bound with them, and those who are ill-treated, since you are also in the body. Let marriage be held in honor among all, and let the bed be undefiled; but God will judge the sexually immoral and adulterers.*

*Be free from the love of money, content with such things as you have, for he has said, "I will in no way leave you, neither will I in any way forsake you."*

*So that with good courage we say,*

*"The Lord is my helper. I will not fear.
What can man do to me?"*

Teach me, O Lord, to follow your commands, and I will follow them to the end. Give me understanding, and I will keep your law and obey it with all my heart.

Direct me in the path of your commands, for there I find delight. Turn my heart toward your word, and not towards selfish gain. Turn my eyes away from worthless things, to the works you have set before me. Grant that I might obey you faithfully all the days of my life.

I know that you will never leave me; or forsake me. I know that you are my helper, and that no matter what circumstances might befall me, I need not be afraid.

O God, give me grace to love my brothers. I want my live to be characterised by your love, and hospitality toward all. Help me to trust in you for my every need, and always be content with what you give me.

Grant that I might always be faithful in my marriage, in my thoughts and deeds. Help me to be a blessing to my family. You, O Lord, are the same yesterday, today and forever. In you I will put my trust, for you are my steadfast Rock, my firm Foundation, and my eternal King. Amen.

# Offer up a sacrifice of praise
## Hebrews 13:7-16

*Remember your leaders, men who spoke to you the word of God, and considering the results of their conduct, imitate their faith.*

*Jesus Christ is the same yesterday, today, and forever. Don't be carried away by various and strange teachings, for it is good that the heart be established by grace, not by food, through which those who were so occupied were not benefited.*

*We have an altar from which those who serve the holy tabernacle have no right to eat. For the bodies of those animals, whose blood is brought into the holy place by the high priest as an offering for sin, are burned outside of the camp.*

*Therefore Jesus also, that he might sanctify the people through his own blood, suffered outside of the gate. Let's therefore go out to him outside of the camp, bearing his reproach.*

*For we don't have here an enduring city, but we seek that which is to come. Through him, then, let's offer up a sacrifice of praise to God continually, that is, the fruit of lips which proclaim allegiance to his name. But don't forget to be doing good and sharing, for with such sacrifices God is well pleased.*

Father, teach me to offer sacrifices of praise. Continually. Open my eyes to your glory that no matter what I am going through, my heart might always be lifted up in thanksgiving.

Help me to do good, and to share everything you have given me, with others. I want to be an example for other believers to imitate.

Give me grace to grow daily in holiness and faithfulness to your word. Strengthen my heart by your grace, that I might walk steadfastly before you, turning neither to the right or the left.

I pray that the work of the cross might ever be before my eyes, reminding me where I have come from, and where I am going to. O Lord my God, may my life be poured out in your service.

I cannot find words to express how much I love you. Your mercy and love is overwhelming. Your power is at constant work in me. Be glorified. Amen.

# May God equip you with every good thing

## Hebrews 13:17-25

*Obey your leaders and submit to them, for they watch on behalf of your souls, as those who will give account, that they may do this with joy, and not with groaning, for that would be unprofitable for you.*

*Pray for us, for we are persuaded that we have a good conscience, desiring to live honorably in all things. I strongly urge you to do this, that I may be restored to you sooner.*

*Now may the God of peace, who brought again from the dead the great shepherd of the sheep with the blood of an eternal covenant, our Lord Jesus, make you*

*complete in every good work to do his
will, working in you that which is well
pleasing in his sight, through Jesus
Christ, to whom be the glory forever and
ever. Amen.*

*But I exhort you, brothers, endure the
word of exhortation; for I have written to
you in few words. Know that our brother
Timothy has been freed, with whom, if he
comes shortly, I will see you.*

*Greet all of your leaders and all the
saints. The Italians greet you.*

*Grace be with you all. Amen.*

Thank you Lord for the leaders in my church. I lift
them up before you and pray that you will strengthen
them by the power of your Spirit.

Give them grace and wisdom and equip them for
everything you have called them to do. Lord, I want
to be a joy to my leaders, not a burden.

Help me to find ways that I might serve, and bless
them, and your church. Protect them from every fiery
dart of the enemy, so that your church might be
blessed and uplifted.

Lord Jesus, you walk among us, tending and looking after your people. Continue to lead and guide us. Open our ears and eyes to your word and your works.

Let us ever walk in obedience to your word, so that men might be drawn to you. In Jesus name I ask, amen.

***

And now dear reader, this is my prayer for you:

*May the God of peace, who through the blood of the eternal covenant brought back from the dead our Lord Jesus, that great Shepherd of the sheep, equip you with everything good for doing his will, and may he work in you what is pleasing to him, through Jesus Christ, to whom be glory for ever and ever. Amen.*

# What's next?

You've reached the end of *Daily Prayer Drawing Near the Throne of Grace.*

So now what?

How about praying through:

- *Daily Prayer Seeking the Heart of God. or*
- *Daily Prayer Pursuing Holiness?*

Or one of these next two books that take you on a prayer journey through another whole book of the Bible?

- Daily Prayer through the Life of Jesus (*Luke*)
- Daily Prayer Taking up the Shield of Faith (*Ephesians*)

Just do a search for *Berenice Aguilera*, and you will find them easily.

\*\*\*

If you like to write down Bible verses and prayers, you might enjoy using this set of journals.

BLACK JOURNAL FOR WOMEN                    BLACK JOURNAL FOR MEN

Taking the time to write out scripture, slowing everything down by thinking, and maybe studying the verses, before praying through them will make a big difference, both to growing in the knowledge of God, and drawing close to Him.

ORANGE FLOWER SERIES                    PARCHMENT SERIES

In each journal there is a page to write out a short Bible passage, followed by a page for reflection on what you have read and written, and a page for your prayers.

Once you have gone through the whole journal, you will have written, thought, and prayed through the whole of at least one book of the Bible.

Each journal comes in a choice of four covers and the series includes all New Testament books. Two with plain interiors, and two with a more detailed design.

These journals are easily found by searching for *Berenice Aguilera Journals.*

Printed in Great Britain
by Amazon